salmonpoetry

Diverse Voices from Ireland and the World

Also by Lex Runciman

POETRY

Salt Moons: Poems 1981-2016
(Salmon Poetry)

One Hour That Morning
(Salmon Poetry)

Starting from Anywhere
(Salmon Poetry)

Out of Town
(Cloudbank Books)

The Admirations
(Lynx House Press)

Luck
(Owl Creek Press)

NON-FICTION

Open Questions
(with Chris Anderson)

Asking Questions: A Rhetoric for the Intellectual Life
(with Chris Anderson)

A Forest of Voices
(with Chris Anderson)

Northwest Variety
(with Steven Sher)

Where We Are: The Montana Poets Anthology
(with Richard Robbins)

Unlooked For

LEX RUNCIMAN

Published in 2022 by
Salmon Poetry
Cliffs of Moher, County Clare, Ireland
Website: www.salmonpoetry.com
Email: info@salmonpoetry.com

ISBN 978-1-915022-12-7

Cover Image: *Sam Roxas-Chua, used by permission of the artist – www.samroxaschua.com*
Cover Design & Typesetting: *Siobhán Hutson*

Printed in Ireland by Sprint Print

to D. J. B. R. for all that 50 years have brought

The four-leaved pattern of a quarter hour
unfolds its conundrum; oh what
will the day bring? What, when the bells
ring evening, will we remember?
Of hours and quarter hours, which
will be honey-tongued? Which echo
in the stroke of all hours forever?

—Mary Barnard

No one can fathom what happens between
a human being and written language.

—Barry Lopez

CONTENTS

Song of Bowl and Cup

cup of anger   cup of sleep
bowl of honey   bowl of grief

cup of water   bowl of blossoms
cup of whisky   bowl of sky

cup to be shunned   bowl to be shared
bowl to be set down

cup of justice   cup of want
bowl to be set down

cup of ochre   cup of glass
bowl of the nest of blue eggs

song of bowl   cup of song
absent one   the other will do

Words That Cannot Now Be Sung

The meadow we walked was bonnie
      down to a green blue sea
before all was changed…

      Still, yes, the meadow bloomed,
reseeded, froze. The sea in its moony tides
      yet raged or dozed,

though what had happened
      numbed us, shock and its weary ache—
and fear, sadness, rage uncheered us,

      clamorous days, new worry and disbelief.
Old questions twist yet unanswered.
      New ones pound our doors,

each loved and troubled face
      its worth now unsayable more.

A Margin of Trust

Between voice and story,
that place a child might seek
beside a parent reading. Against illness,
hope's memory of health. Goodwill
that cancels offence or disregard, as
between me and you the presumptions
and actions of decency, a willingness
to question and listen—a margin of trust.

And some rare days entire, dark to dark,
it's call and response, plan and action, no hitch
in the breath only ease—a cloudless, October,
wind-aided day, horizon's bend gentle,
waves shallow, the tide out far, each step
in that sand-wide dry a shift and slide
that squelches, gives, then bottoms—
rock below, all emptiness of blue above,

and in it, held and restless in its own margin,
a kite painted with two huge eyes,
the tether string soon invisible,
so a hovering of restless unblinking
above a swaying length
of thin, knotted-fabric tail—a vigilance
aloft and curious to gulls,
as we take turns holding on.

If the Forecast Holds

If the forecast holds, this rainy spell
will lead to an infrequent snow, all colors white
and all shapes softened, pristine in a blue dawn.
A new year will see birthdays, new divorces,

broken bones, hearts opened, hearts closed.
Raspberries will fruit and apples ripen, green
or speckled or red, and one late September evening,
windows open, someone will be singing,

operatically, even the crows gone still.
This and more will occur as foretold, until the last day,
when every bit of it slips unknown to the disappearing
and final past—though of course here we are,

you and I, listening or reading, listening, reading,
looking up from the words even now.

Picture Too Large to See

—*Las Meninas, 1656*

Archaic, monumental—
this canvas Diego Velazquez court painter and subject
has painted himself into, wherein he has just stepped back,
a palette of wet colors in hand as now he studies us,
as though we might yet be part of his subject
on that canvas twice his height,
held by two stretchers taut in its frame.

We see what he's not painting.
He stands in a room, airy and high, figures to his left
resplendent in the lace and frills of the Spanish court.
Royal and God-anointed is the center-front girl,
her ivory gown best lit by the window right, her days
no spontaneity, no wish unmet, and no one could know
how young she would die. Commentators will tell you
who is who and what what, but really it's too tall,
too wide to see all at once. You have to face it,
let haste go slack—you have to choose how to look:
what's not there, what is, this person or that,
the way an intricate ribbon in bows attaches a sleeve,
a conversation you'll never hear, a sated dog,
farther back, a door, a stair, someone coming, going,
ever turned to see who you are.

Nine feet across and ten feet tall,
a painting like this must have asked days, months
of patience, mixed colors, attention to space, shadow,
object, detail, each brush-stroke a decision
to make, unmake… *Better*, Velazquez thinks.
Palette set down, soon he will need to eat.
He rolls his shoulders, goes outside, looks up:
lead white, bone black, red ochre, azurite blue.

What Do You Carry?

—Oregon Humanities call for writers

Beaches and their weather,
       how sand in seasons moves—
how walking just north of the cove
       I know inches below that summer's curve
cold basalt stretches flat, gray seamed,
       uneven swirled, ancient and stolid
yet somehow under January windless sun
       jaunty as a wind-caught cap
pinwheeling into August's surfy dissipations.

*

My seven-year-old fingers carry black
       pitted olives, Thanksgiving, a mother
too kitchen-busy to scold me then, father
       into his second drink, or third, that dark
mahogany dressed in white silvery silken
       linen, and plated, glassed, knived,
forked and spooned, gravy-bowled, salt-cellared
       and pepper-shakered, formal,
terrifying—a three inch phone book on my chair,
       all joints on the table will be carved.
Also years of rains on roofs, that sound in sleep,
       storm of the five days, candles,
no school. And whom would you kill,
       and whom would you disobey?

*

Hospital corridors know me uncomforted,
       that April morning dewy-clear, first
he'd never see. Birds know me, and slugs, deer,
       hissy possums, raccoons and skunks.

The silence of a cougar once, its large paws, lilting
       tail, and coyotes baying at sirens.
(Ask not what has been lost, forgot, set down.)
       Creek water cold. Window views.
Fir trees' night silhouettes. Two Chevrolets,
       a land boat Buick, blood on snow.
And births, simple, thankful, agonized, indelible,
       fears gone and fears thus bestowed, gifts
loved—not, not ever to be set down.
       With America's two original sins,
luck and privilege are what I carry.
       And in marriage, oh such company.

"Life is, Soberly and Accurately, the Oddest Affair"

—*Virginia Woolf*

With Mrs. Dalloway
we walked London streets and parks, remarked
        on flowers, heard the chiming hours sound,
and found the blue-plaque Stephens house.
        And from the hill of Talland House, St. Ives,
we saw her same view down—a girl at the window
        that day more interested in sky than bay.

We saw the River Ouse curve swift and deep—
we crossed it on a swing bridge at the Southease stop.
        Through hay fields then, a slender road up
past the tiny church unlocked, and so the path
        to Rodmell, food at the one pub there,
and then to the house, the room Virginia and Leonard
        and so many others sat at supper,
low beams, tile floor, Vanessa's paintings (a harbor,
        a portrait) on the walls.

Yes, we found the outdoor loo, and
having entered the room with her bed amid all its books,
        from its green door we followed bricks
to zinnias, red asters, mums—September's garden
        profusion overgrown, the orchard, clipped lawn
for bowls, the lodge she wrote in, cliffs in the distance
        white as she knew. By the dew pond, with lilies,
quick colors, a gentle breeze, we sat on a bench.
        And last, resolved
to better get thought and feeling right,
        we walked the stubble fields back.

Letter to Rutsala from Sellwood

Dear Vern,
You've been gone years now, longer than the house
next door, demolished bite by backhoe hydraulic bite—
ancient knob and wire, its lead and leaky pipes,
fissured concrete, stick walls, gable ends
snapped, pummeled, loaded into the troughs of trucks.
That was months ago. Now, rains back, that dirt's gone
to green weeds and burrowed holes squirrels have dug
for walnuts and hazelnuts buried ceaselessly
and without maps. I have been reading your little book,
Other Voices—Translations and Variations, you knowing
it's all and always just that: translating, and singing
the given variations. Your absence registers here,
your rooms conjured and gone, lone evenings
into darkness, sleep unwilling, old walls and memory
settling in their joins, rock plaster, rafters, sill and joists,
and you deep in a chair, or sat at your kitchen table,
wondering again how you got there, how any of us
get anywhere—when it started, how to live it,
when it might end, how the best questions stay.

Obsidian Snow

Where The Clearances pushed them
                    to heather, saltwater,
the rock and wrack of Loch Duich,
they built dark houses of stacked stone,
            and the narrow rows of seaweed
—that cold slick mess by their hands dredged
                    and arranged to decompose—
those rows have been called *lazybeds*.

No dark houses here,
                    though in Lake County,
Glass Buttes make an obsidian snow of flakes,
                            gray to black,
the ancient shard and cast-offs
of blade making, scraper, arrowhead, spear—
            patient labor
no lies, disease, massacre, or treaty or policy
has ever silenced.

And so with caves, desert washes, playas,
                        and painted hills,
with alders, fir, hemlock and cedar,
columnar basalt by great waters gouged
                    and cold creeks scoured,
and north canyon slopes snow-greened
                        all the way to August,
that raw historic Anglo complicity comes to me—

easy cut, quick blood,
        the slick and dazzle of glass.

This Crazy Old Home

*—Oregon Wildfires Burn
Over 1,000,000 Acres*

Mossy boulders:
pull off that layer, and you hold
uncountable days and nights,
　　　this creek's oxygen muscle and tumble,
how May and June and August own no names
but bird calls, light's angle,
　　　the slower drop and trickle
that is September,

and later, those dull days, sun lost
　　　　　　　in drizzling rain,
sun that hardly rises above the rim, those mosses
turn then determined and serious,
　　　all the wet-green capillaries swollen,
snowed over, thawed, happy as they will be ever,
all ooze and drip with all they cannot keep.

Hot days, burdened, tired,
intent on destination, I have walked past such places,
or stopped, sat on such boulders
　　　where mosses made a thickest cushion, sat
and picked at twigs, ate a sandwich—
　　　　　　　　ten minutes
here or there, no agenda,
assuming all of it would and will be forever.

Winter in the Pandemic Years

Even as we are each to each made alien,
yet soon in dogwood geranium time
bees in vine maples will hover and inquire

as cirrus fleet and thin in deep, quiet blue.
In shadowed pools, trout will gill and hold
against sun that would glint them obvious to hawks.

Pollen will go washed in rain. A ginger fox
will sun itself asleep in the root bole of a birch.

This day and this week, the deaths will be
individual and without recompense, the grief
a stunning—inconsolable. And yet, and yet,

two brave people, reckless, promised, true,
marry today—nothing clearer to them
or more impossible to say.

Reading the *Autobiography*
of William Carlos Williams

Biography's hard, autobiography is story,
a poem makes the possible… So, winter,

1918, his gray suit spotted with powders,
Dr. William Carlos Williams makes house calls,
60 a day if we can believe him—strep, croup,
mostly flu, a killer traveling, he half thinks,
in his own instrument bag.

He knows fever and worry flare at 3am.
Knuckles or a fist on his door, or his phone rings—
they believe, they want to believe, he can stop it.
Names of days, when he ate last, slept in a bed
or knew anything but weak hearts, bad eyes,
lymph nodes the size of plums—he loses track.

"I lost two young women in their early twenties,"
he says. Some nights listening to breathing, he nods off
in the sick room chair, until the coughing starts again.
What he can do is not enough.

He rubs his face, turns to a gray window: chickens,
a wheelbarrow, rain. "The epidemic over," he says,
"April, 1918, was as lovely as ever."

Unlooked For

Dinner table cleared, my father's place empty,
we're outside, my brother and me, as the phone rings,
and from the screen door our mother alive calls to us
your father's on his way, which we can hardly believe—
meet him at the corner, she says, and tilts her head, *Go on.*

So, obedient as we were then, Bruce and I,
we run to that corner by a neighbor's apple boughs
propped up with 2 x 4s, and we stand there
until an older convertible never seen by us before
stops a block away, top down, and it's our father
driving one-handed, cigarette that will kill him,
face in an Elvis pout. We wave. He doesn't.
Maybe he'll just drive on, but he stops, and we clamor over
and in, *keep going*, we tell him, *anywhere, we don't care.*
And he does, and when we get back—this I love—
his wife says to him, *well*, and, *what have you done now?*

… Unlooked for, what moment and memory give—
Bobby Kennedy on a flatbed truck in the dark:
he says *Martin Luther King has been shot in Memphis*,
and that crowd gasps—but they listen to someone
whose brother was also killed by a white man.
And it is a difficult day, he says, a difficult time
for the United States. *We can do well in this country*, he says.

And one day my father's used car filled with water,
top down in a downpour, the rest of us elsewhere,
while inside he napped on the couch.

Amherst

I read a sunny afternoon,
window raised, a quiet Amherst room,

Emily Dickinson's, hers, upstairs,
where once she wrote *my business*

is to love, and where she thought Death
kindly stopped. And though I know the grieved

are many, yet a wild fierce presence lives,
a welcome to any flower, bird, or bee,

and so to any fellow human, a promise
of all the intricate moves of justice—

to Breonna Taylor and George Floyd,
Trayvon Martin and Sandra Bland,

to Armaud Arbery and Dominique Fells,
Philando Castile and Elijah McClain,

these and too, too many more,
and Emmett Till, killed when I was four.

Eventually You See Your Childhood

God knows how she put up with us except she loved God.
Religion confuses me now, but I do believe she said to herself
daily, *I love God.* As she dressed in the folds of her habit,
she said *I love this drab and unpromising morning and*

give it to God. God this and that all day. God in the janitor
who slicked the floor, the volunteer parent with cancer,
the lay Tuesday librarian who would not meet her gaze,
the Wednesday librarian whose makeup covered a bruise.

God in the petty and caustic priest who terrified
those he might otherwise molest. God in the small persons
who lost lunches, tripped on their own laces, and could not
keep a shirt tucked in, boys who threw chalk, masticated

paper and flicked spitwads that splat on the board and stuck
whenever she turned her back, whenever she wrote—
and they worked so hard again when she looked, all but one,
God love him, no sense or shame: he'd see her scowl,

and grin. *God preserve my virtuous anger,* she said to herself
before scolding the tardy, the selfish, the enraged, the sullen
and the hurt. *God preserve each of these 49 children—
the boy who reads comics during arithmetic, the girl*

*with the spastic stomach, the tuna-fish-sandwich boy,
girls with early breasts, the smart who wish they were not,
and the twins, last in a line of eight, always hungry.*
September gives her children she will love.

She cries in June, and thanks God they are gone.

2.

And now I see the faces we did not see.
Indigenous faces, that long heritage of salmon,
        of coyote and raven, story and resistance—
our guilt history unspoken, unheard.
        Seats empty, too, of those whose parents
picked by the pound summer bings, peaches,
        red apples, sweet onions, melons, and pears,
and those whose grandparents or parents knew
        the arid dust camps at Minidoka or Tule Lake.

And not one childhood dark face or family story.
        No explanation how a human body
could ever be legal property, nor how for 77 years
        our constitution could say such persons
denied on our shores, under Oregon skies.
        Mist, drizzle, steady, and downpour,
and there we sit, the never-present ungrappled with
        and at home.

Laundry

No color, no pocket—undershirts we called them,
                     common as salmon, soft new pristine,
given later to slack-ribbing around the neck
         and by one or another—berries or grass—stained,
or by splots of blood metallic red that never quite washed out.
         And there's the T poles and lines they dry on,
a pouch of wooden, steel-sprung pins
               for blouses and boxers,
tidy whiteys, bras, and handkerchief squares,
         shifts and flannels, kitchen towels muslin,
a rose-blush terry-cloth robe hung by limp and footless socks.
            Bed linens last, sheets not linen at all
but cotton—great stiff and flapping sails to hide among
         or hide behind, one with a toenail hole:
hold breath, squint, look out, don't touch.

Homage to Norman Maclean

Water haunted me early,
Lazy burn mud slow in summer slack,
But in full-runneled winter into spring
A quick rising under firs, maples, a briar tangle
Walkable from home.

God it was cold as it ran downhill,
Up the wrist as I bent spraddle-legged over
To reach down and first touch whatever it was
Made by lean water out of focus
But ever-present, white appearing, lines,

Veins iron brown then white again,
And, another shock, not smooth but jagged
As some ancient continuous bone.
About this I said nothing, showed no one.
I alone knew this secret and mystery

And solid fact, a clarity I could touch—
If my balance kept. Season on season
I knew this, then didn't go back for decades
After the bulldozers came, memory
Not gone but present, a hillside wood,

Spring water in a twisty line
Bottomed by a seam of quartz,
Water clear pure
In that jam glass I'd stolen
And hid there for my thirst.

Whiskey and a Slice of Pie—

That's her, 1962,
Though she'd hate my saying so.
Early Times, the phrasing I remember—
Early Times Mist, a vodka martini for dad,
Two, maybe three, before the entrees arrive,
And we, my brother and I, yet learning

To wait, sit, not fidget—
Restaurant manners matter.
And on July 4th, the pie was apple, usually,
Rhubarb, sometimes, as she favored—
The key for us of course, sugar, sweetness,
Not bourbon's bite.

Summer at last. With soapy water
We have brushed the redwood table clean.
Cigarette lit, first drink in hand, she loves us more,
And any pie with ice cream comes welcome.
Whiskey. Slice of pie. Screen door
She backs open with her hip—

She's carrying a bowl-and-plate-laden tray.
I miss her. There she is.

Loving Beer

This night one for thirst.
And this night one against regret.
And this tomorrow for the crescent spirea,
White wind waving, bloom mostly gone.

And there rests a Blitz on a redwood bench—
Brown stubby so dark when you look in
No beer is there, only that lager and hop
Sweet bitterness of stolen, quick gulps
While the four of us tidied the yard
Of spent ferocious bloom.

One last now for shears and rakes
And wooden-handled trowels set down,
And leather, sweat-soaked gloves
Drying in the shape of hands.

This Day

You can tell from of the wires overhead
And the two-horse coach coming on,
Electricity's there, but not yet the car.

Color of cream now, this 1890 snow.
Snow in the air. Deciduous branches
Bare laden, likely elm, likely long since

Victims of blight. White street, white
Sidewalk, boardwalk, empty field lot.
Two blocks distant, two storeys, a bell—

Someone taught in that school, the upper
And lower grades. That false front's lost its sign.
Consumption, ague, polio, flux, grippe.

Slow hymns in the bell-towered church.
Someone owned the brick building
With the awning starting to fill. This day

Looking out, they all talked of snow.
That blur is a cap-headed boy,
Cold or late or both, hurrying by.

Seamus Heaney, St. Mary's, Bellaghy

You being gone now, vanished
And everywhere, we find you
And fail to find you, grave and marker
Inside the fence, just—
Closer to field than to nave or door.
Others have brought stones

As I see now I could have,
Basalt made oval, say, multiply concussed
By that ever surge and wash
Below Yaquina Head light, a far offering,
Small ballast against a squally morning.
But no. Empty-handed,

I squat down at your feet
To read, to speak, the words
In your mouth first, *Walk on air
Against your better judgement.*
There. I have said them aloud
Because you did and now cannot.

Night's rains over, torn clouds hurrying,
And I turn away glad in my heart.

Faltering Spring

Now the pink and white and last salmon dogwoods
        unclench, un-fist,
and tiny uncountable lanterns of maples
        open, dust and drift golden underfoot.
Age, a heavy-taloned bird,
        mutters and sleeps on my shoulder, startles,
re-grips—it does not like
        what the black-headed grosbeak sings.

Today, unaccountably why—
        Virginia Woolf says nothing I can hear,
nor Elizabeth Bishop, nor Dickinson,
        nor Whitman, Brooks, Morrison, nor Keats.
Let go, head says. Walk farther, feet say.
        This stone from Oaks Bottom,
grasp and heft it as memory: tall firs, a summer day,
        your brother coasting a bicycle downhill,

you plodding yourself halfway up, his shape oncoming.
        He laughs going by,
shouts something, leans back, feet splayed,
        both his hands waving.

Keeping It All

Here are named and described the kinds, ranges, and diets
of penguin, here the ascending order of clouds, here
nine species of ants with the preferred habitat of each.

These pages illustrate the designs of medieval furniture, principally
Germanic and Persian, chairs and stools, their materials, widths
and heights. Here, the doves consumed from a rural dovecot, Sussex,
1638-1641, all recorded in a volume handbound in calf in 1642.

These illustrations depict in watercolors twenty separate tulips,
a page for each. These, three faces of bats, and these, eight species
of fish shorter than a finger.

These hands, each drawn from life, belong to a tanner, a smith,
a lace-maker, a wheelwright, a milk maid, a carter, and a nun.
Here at half-scale you see the footprints of an Asian elephant,
a cougar, a pea fowl, raccoon, lemur, river otter, and heron.

Also drawn from life are these fifteen depictions of the webs of spiders,
and three African birds: the black-crowned crane, a yellow-casqued
hornbill, and a kingfisher, orange-beaked, smaller than a fist.

This last is a sewn book of citrus—each double-page with woodcuts:
characteristic bloom, the fruit shown whole, then in cross-section,
above italic text for growing season, and water asked for weekly
in measure with the trunk's circumference one foot above the earth.

Neap Tide

Those first weeks, his death made an insistence
                            to muscle through—
taking a shower, sleeping,
                    trying to sleep, the half refuge of work.
And though grief's injustice varied
                            as light varies
with June cumulus and wind,
                it would neither be shed nor shifted
as a suitcase is set down and picked up again
                            with the other hand.
In an album
            packed in a box I do not wish to open,
its last-filled, black-paper pages
                            hold our first days,
eight photos each, eight grades—
                his first through my twelfth,
the coats on our backs a cousin's, then mine, then his,
        all of them gray,
dates in white in our mother's cursive hand.
                            His grin, that happiness,
its brevity—as adults, we hardly spoke.
            Adopted (we had that in common),
no one mistook us for brothers.

The day's only sun comes through late and low,
                    between horizon and overcast,
backlighting each wave
                    pale green to blue curl and fall,
blue curl and fall
            no language fixes nor beauty stays.

Let Me Tell You

Sometimes you want to sit on a porch.
Or, if you have no porch,
sometimes you want to invent one.

And it need not be the widest veranda,
could be concrete, small as it is, west-facing,
open to the south. And you can sit

in one of the two chairs—June to September
a bake oven, but in the shoulder months
a warmth might rise on your trousers and coat

and so bring back a lake surface,
blinding-brilliant to look at straight on
from the back of that boat you have rowed out,

watching the dock slowly go distant
against all those shore firs. Old bilge water sloshes
warm on your bare feet. And in such wide quiet

you're glad for your legs and shoulders.
Glad for your eyes, for distance,
and the bill of your cap.

Glad you have learned how to row like this,
how to scull a circle
and so take your time rowing home.

To Know This Your Home

Turn awhile from all things other.
That maple at the corner goes fire early.
November fog vanishes the farther oaks
Even as those nearer ones gnarl
As though growth itself hurts.
In spring rains, two wood ducks settle
The russet, blue, white, black, quick
Brown and viridian creek. In wide-opened July,
Just west of that chimney, Jupiter appears.
To know this your home, turn a full circle slow.
Touch fingers and thumb with fingers and thumb.
Under December's last round moon,
Praise all clouds gone: on breath made steam,
Name who holds you, whom you hold.

Oranges Shared

Then that spring-to-summer near our door,
one aged orange tree made bloom on the air:
flower and scent to smallest fruit to green-

skinned and lemon tart, those branches
ever deeper-arced, until a mild sweetness
piqued the bitter. And slow days later

the bitter become oranges as we'd known them,
then sudden-sugared as never had we known them,
oranges iconic, oranges Platonic—any meal,

too many, we could not not eat them,
skins fragile then, fermentation exquisite,
and last a heaven of wasps and birds,

a wreckage of rinds and rot.
Leaves went. Rains came. The roof leaked.
And from work or late errand come back

in the dark (that light over the rented stoop
ever shorted out), we elbowed and jostled
to push open the one stuck door...

Now, quiet out, sun up, just, as he peels
a clementine, little citric fountains
at fingers and thumb,

globed fruits sectioned, one of them, two,
half a century of mornings, she walks in,
says, *My nose tells me oranges.*

Eyes and Hand

—Four photos of Joan Eardley, painter, circa 1955

She sketches in pastel a neighbor Glasgow boy
       wearing a onesie and eating a sweet
almost too large to grip. Hair askew as when he woke,
       he's frowning at the camera—
only that sweet's keeping him on the seat.

But here he's looking at her and she at him—
       you can trace the line—as he sits
on a wooden, too-large chair
       and she leans in from a low bench, board on her lap
and her hand at work, eyes and hand,
       eyes and hand. He smiles watching her face,
each of them smiling—she's familiar
       and he likes her.

And in her mid-30s here, she stands in a field
       near Catterline, Scotland, nice enough day,
no clouds, windy though—you can tell
       by her short, blown hair—and she holds the easel
that it might not topple. Paint, not a lot,
       on her canvas pullover—she has rolled the sleeves,
and her face says get on with it please.

Last: a rocky shore, close ocean heave and churn.
       She's rope-weighted the easel with a stone
large as a bucket. Even so, the wind must have slacked
       because that canvas five feet by four
would otherwise sail. Paint cans open at her feet,
       her back's to us, soaked beret, saggy coat,
left hand in a pocket, the right with a brush held out:
       she has paused to take it all in again—
an hour as impossible to catch as any child.

On First Seeing a Photo of My Birth Mother

Somewhere not here, wherever she is,
if she is—for I would like her to be
in earshot, though none could speak so loud—

I would greet her on my birthday.
She would wake from that one day's
thin bed of necessity and loss, another year passed,

and she would think of the unborn
she carried, spoke to, shifting a pointy heel
or elbow away from her bladder,

not there, little one, and *stay awhile, stay*—

and when she thinks of that infant
she birthed into Earth's air,
heard cry and held most briefly and gave away, away,

at that very moment she would see me,
and I her, and from my pocket I would take a pear,
and from another pocket a folding knife

to quarter that fruit and ease the pips aside,
and she would peel for us both a tangerine
and in each of us offering the other half,

our hands would touch.

News, 1949

And so she poured the clear libation
       over the rattle and cracking welcome
           of cubes of ice,

and with soda watered that liquid,
       and for herself opened an amber bottle
           and in the same fashion poured

in that one expectation of the happiest of effects,
       and soon those glasses filmed with thinnest fog
           as the air warmed.

The life we have made is good, she thinks to herself,
       the kitchen fire well caught now, alive
           in darkened windows, white and red

and yellow. Their table set, candles in place, the plates,
       knives, the four-tined forks, and by now,
           by steady sips her first glass has emptied—

she pours a second, even then turning
       as she hears a car motor arrive and switch off,
           a door opening, a door closing, footsteps,

and she is poised, ready, calm.

Himself

—John Angus MacDonald, South Uist,
Hebrides, 1954, photo by Paul Strand

He could have been me, but he isn't,
this boy in his large-buttoned, long,
    tattered-sleeved shirt,

a warm enough day, shoeless as he is,
    short pants sewn from an old towel,
one foot on a stone

    as he stands with sedges and grass
against a rock-stacked wall.
    Who is this stranger wanting his picture,

not that he cares, he's on an errand,
    no hurry to finish, a small creek to cross—
he'll use that sturdy stick his left hand rests on,

    this day in 1954,
when he believes all his future has been decided,
    though none of it has…

    He thinks no more of it
until he's retired, and his daughter or her daughter
    takes him to a gallery,

where around a corner he recognizes a boy,
    that one, framed on a wall,
and though much comes back,

    he cannot believe that was himself.

Lines Composed after Four Days of Steady Rain

"A very rainy morning."
"Very rainy all the morning."
"A very rainy, or rather showery and gusty morning."
"A rainy day."

DOROTHY WORDSWORTH, Dove Cottage, Grasmere, October, 1800

A complicated place, the past—
it tasks us: be other, and better. Design by sun,
    by leaf and feather, morel, chanterelle, and bee,
and finback, right, gray, bottlenose, and sperm.
    Make habit not for profit's catastrophe
but story ongoing, as now this gray iambic rain
    reminds me of Grasmere, its little green square
sodden, St Oswald's yews and churchyard sodden,
    the River Rothay's risen sound hurrying past
the Wordsworth graves—William's and Sarah's,
    sister Dorothy, daughter Dora,
and Thomas, age 6, Catherine, ever not yet quite 4.
    And though it's not exactly the bliss of solitude,
nor emotion in tranquility recollected,
    you can in words and fact go there,
walk that rocky track to Rydal under rain,
    trees shedding, flat water pewter, brief silver,
the stone you awkward tread a channel braided
    loud with what gathers and waterfalls—
such trail the Wordsworths and Coleridge knew—
    waxed canvas coats, who knows what sewn shoes.
On rock not far distant they carved initials
    formal as cut lead, and sat nearby in sun,
and tried, each and together, to listen,
    intuit, look and think and say
what time had brought them—a moment, this,
    the next, how earth reveals itself in cloud,

rain, sun, chill, warm; in leaf shape, oak poise,
      heathered, brackened, slaty ground,
and fruit seeds in a green linnet gut—
      such admirations found, born into,
their conversation not science merely,
      nor sympathy, nor philosophy nor health,
but all of these, *beauty*—until at last they sat quieted.
      Clouds blew in. Leaving apple cores for birds,
they started back, not as they had come,
      failing, minutes later, to out-walk the rain
then, which is not and is this rain and ours.
      So the past that tasks us may love us yet.

Axis and Spin

Suppers, breakfasts, the dark
a long cold dark, sometimes friendly, sometimes a comfort,

yet winter—winter's dark a long cold dark.

Then birds, birds in the foredawn, sky
clear, early sun like something from Ravel, unfurling

(though pollutants lodge in the lobes of our lungs,
and always that violence about what is or is not holy).

And this morning as any morning at my desk a plaster copy
of the life mask of John Keats greets me in sun so slant new

it lights the understory.

Eyes closed, mouth closed, cheeks and forehead
greased and plaster-soaked, wheat straws
in his nostrils... He writes a note: how long?

Ten minutes, someone says, ten minutes more.
People talk, he hears them shift in their chairs...

Axis and spin, this first warm morning
every surface blinding bright, like plaster pulled away—

John Keats, John Keats, open your eyes.

Keats

1. IN WINCHESTER

"I take a walk every day for an hour before dinner"

—JOHN KEATS, *letter to George Keats, September 17-27, 1819*

This time, for a change,
        not the river meadows, but the High Street
up the hill, sky white cloud and blue,
                        love of distance
or his afflicted lungs prompting him to pause,
turn, take in the view—
                cathedral spires to St. Giles Hill,
late summer calm into autumn, taking it in.

So he passes under the West Gate,
and up yet to the Great Hall, circa 1235—
                of the castle only this remaining.
Inside, flint heights,
        an oak-beamed and distant roof,
all the while Arthur's table 12 foot round,
medieval, a red eye on the wall.
                        Old place.
Before he turns,
he touches a column of Purbeck marble,
cool and still.

2. AT 80

Had he longer lived, beech trees turning
Would have longer known him,
As would in Margate the long slow swells
Arriving under a wind-driven, white-clouded blue.
Museums would have known him
A tiny old man, arthritic knees, the patience

Required to navigate a gallery, pausing
At the case with the bog shoe, that leather
Browned deep, tannin kept, design
Yet picked out heel to toe above the sole,
With stitches tight and the toe upturned
As by the pattern shaped—

And then the maker's eyes
And hands that stretched that leather,
Cut and matched, a pair, gut sewn, trimmed,
The once-painted red embellishments become delight
At such a gift—a young girl first wearing them,
Looking down, turning, walking out a door . . .

This in less than a minute
As he rested two-handed on a hazelwood knob,
His imagination yet the sort such made things
Caught on, like fleece strands on a thorny bush,
Or mud on a common brogue—
One of those awkward hugs in the rain.

Gold Beach

—for Jordan, Aran, Jacob, and James

The plan an hour, a saunter, low tide,
mist on skin, shine in the air—Hunter Creek
and back, maybe some keeper stones.

*

One agate, smallest amber, knobbed, lucent,
thick as your thumb.

*

This rounded heft in your palm—basalt
seamed by dirty white quartz
pocked like suet a bird's been at.

*

This one all quartz, a matchbox aslant,
fracture lines like pin scratch.

*

And last, this thinnest green, one side
dark as the inner pokey reaches of a shore pine,
the other marbled bright salmonberry.

*

Four in all and none alike—
an hour's coat-pocket abundance
sent with you in mind

from and for where memory lives
and what you imagine, you see.

He is Two and Does Not Want Shoes

—for Aran

His opposition wriggly and loud
is overcome only by the promise of running.
So at last, shoes on, coat on, laces tight,

we all of us descend the trail to low tide sand
and he is full tilt for a rooty stump and trunk,
its length, bulk, and intricate height

stranded by storm. Redwood or cedar,
debarked, gouged, salt slicked as it is,
yet unfalteringly he climbs

to the tallest gnarly height, taller than we are,
balances, looks out, looks back, grins,
and before we can stop his puffy jacket bulk

and blur of arms and hair, he leaps
up, out, down, and hits with his feet
and rolls—howling and laughing.

This Time

"Remorse is memory awake—"
EMILY DICKINSON

Less than two minutes—
that's all you'd change. One small,
too-quickly-made decision

you know now tipped the balance
entirely not where you wished, to shock,
then anger you could be so wrong, be

the agent of such wrong. Loud anger.
Tears, your fault, wanting to explain,
even as you knew such error could not be

called back, called back, the injury done.
You did not anticipate.
Maybe to anticipate is not possible,

which fails to dilute the sense
you botched it when you shouldn't have.
And that it's too late now

offers the opposite of consolation—
offers only that ache that is remorse.

Even Now

Warm day, wide sky, deep blue.
Along the top of a stone ruined wall
    twice my height,
leggy weedy plants I cannot name

    have rooted in unseeable declivities,
hollows that have over decades filled, somehow,
    with soil sufficient to green stem
and leaf only rain can water,

    and which now, in the midst
of long days of sweaty heat, have risen
    into carmine blooms—such *fecundity*,
a word the Puritans would aver,

    this ardor, zeal, slow and naked frenzy,
an orchestration, *gratis*, root tip to leaf
    to petal edge, this
leaning as it knows perfectly how
    to the energy that feeds it, even now.

Glance and Look Away

—after the paintings of Ron Mills

No brogue or cup or moonlit pewter tree,
                                but color,
color shading over color into color, line sure,
                    line gone, luxury, yet line,
the eye by intensity urged,
by volume and quiet not quite silence,
                                as though logic itself
has become night snowfall or maple forest light,
                                July light
that, if one could manage the acuity and patience,
could become what always it is:
                                an intricacy
unsayable, and, in its multitude, whole.
                    So glance and look away
and look again to follow an idea entirely optic,
wordless, yet as though reading words,
                        silent, yet a music composed.
After which the world of objects
                    makes welter and surprise—
voice is melody,
and words feel like sight.

New Year: View from the Night Stairs

—Tintern, Wales

By distance made separate
      from memory and from home,
This sun looks not medieval, which this place is,
      but unexampled, cold open as noon,
This place in time and out, unglassed windows,
      no roof but blue.

Climb then the cupped treads,
      the night stairs' chiseled risers:
At the top when you turn,
      a solar physics, not holy not pagan,
Rubs two floor-tombs too slick for script.
      Transept, chancel, aisle and nave,

Every vision is stacked wall,
      shaped column, mortar, shadow,
Green wet gold—steam in the air,
      sun on grass, sun on stone.
This bright unshriven hour, let questions be.
      Birch in a window,

In a valley, by a river.

Ferry from Harris to Skye

A memory rehearsed, so I see it plainly yet.
Glary sun, a windswept day though by the harbor sheltered,
the ferry loading its walkers, its trucks and its cars.

I'm at the stern rail where it's already colder as the engines
thrum and we churn the waters foam blue away, and only then
do I see them, two figures arm in arm on the pier,

a woman in a brown scarf tight-drawn over her hair
—she reminds me of my mother driving the car to church—
together with a stout-coated, taller fellow in a flat cap.

No one else, only the two of them standing at that edge.
Until the woman leans her head as though to speak,
and then first one and then the other raises a gloved hand.

They're waving to someone likely at the rail above me,
or maybe waving only in the hope of someone who will
see them, coffee in hand, from a window on the top deck.

And I do not know if their waving is answered, or, if it's not,
whether they'd feel it a useless gesture. What I can say
is they wave, timidly at first, as though distrusting any excess.

Yet as they diminish in the larger distance, their arms move
faster, the gesture larger, and as we curve around a headland
into that unbounded wind, they stand small and waving.

Beach Walking, Early March, No Hat

"This is the tasteless water of souls."
WALT WHITMAN

In worry's featureless gray he had walked out
and kept on along a margin of shore pines and spruce
leaned because they need to be, and she had walked
quickly, beset entirely by what is or might be
or is surely to come, and he did not think of weather,
how low pressure had hammered and hurled itself
all night's mile by dark hour over water
until that riverous southwest to northeast caught
and shattered sudden across their shoulder
and made on the back of their scalp needle drills
quick to soak and drip, lull and gusts—
rain all the moment, and she's leaning into it,
this ocean's air of voices, all water off nose or brow
swept by wind away, as in that dim morning gray
he turned and started back, sure only
they will ever have done too little to merit this planet
of water and salt, its history, my history,
all souls, all I love, this moment, this.

Hillside at Laugharne

A fine morning after mist has cleared, the far view
Welsh hedges, small pasture, rooks, oaks and elms.

And though on this stony churchyard hill
Dylan Thomas is not here, is not the white cross here,

Yet to sit on this grass is to think of him fondly—
Not his folly, not his poverty, but his outsized wishes—

Language so dense-fitted for mouth and tongue
Sense can disappear and be hardly missed,

Though in their best blest assemblies
Those lines of consonants and vowels conspire

To all the song-clarity ears might bear
And sight know and thought ask, blood and breath

At the moon's one door, mortal, cup-full in its arriving,
And cloudy, starry, lonely in its going away.

Looking for the Story Line

Say it starts on a seacoast, basalt stacks,
sun on that spindrift corona green, cream, pale blue,
                              pink, as wind takes it.
Or the story begins with clay from wet ground dug,
shaped to what a palm can hold, dull weight
thunk on a platter, centered and treadle spun
as fingers and thumbs lift it narrower, taller,
                              hollowed, round,
while the blunt ends of feathers wait
to make pattern in and on that circled cup.

If sun lights the beginning of the story
                    and the beginning of the story is lost,
where must we go but the year's full dark,
as wintered birds to reassure themselves
                              chitter and call,
and on Wednesday evenings far, far elsewhere
—across the great pond—

in Winchester's shuttered, rain-black January,
Wednesdays, 7pm, the novice cathedral bell-ringers
                    in repetitive practice
make startling, unlikely, collective,
bright, over-chiming imperfections.
They practice for summer's dazzle of weddings.
                    They practice happiness.

Annunciations

No theology I can say now, but I do wonder
About Gabriel, the angel, sent unaccustomed to Earth.
   I suppose what he felt had none but human names,
Confusion first among them—the woman with a fresh catch
   Who waved him off—*What would I have to do with you*

With all these fish? The one who looked at him sadly
   And shut the door. The one after another
Who said simply, *no*. He didn't dress like them.
   Some saw wings and doubted their eyes.
And until he got it right, his voice sounded inhuman,

   So that after a day or two, glances would follow him.
What he felt then was either pity or fear.
   One town with a fine harbor held him long enough
He understood the gulls, their single-mindedness.
   When he spoke to them, they leapt into the air.

Who are you, one woman asked. *Gabriel*, he said.
   Go home, Gabriel, she said, *Go home*. He learned
He liked to walk. In a tree's shade, he saw a woman
   And a man, both dying—this he knew.
He sat at a distance. As they made no objection,

   He moved closer. The woman saw him, raised her hand,
Attend my brother, she said. Hours later he buried them both.
   Refused and refused, he wandered. Four tries more
Or fourteen, he lost count. And even heard once and done,
   Relief only woke in him a new melancholy
Of substance, time, taste, and air.

A Watcher's Triptych

Akin to Constable's, these clouds,
great painter of water pastures and cows.
If stranded in Hampstead, look up.

*

Years of nights I have seen her sleep,
the live skin of her cheek in first light
a shape unshadowing, pulse as soft color,
a temple, an ear, this privilege
long assent yet gives.

*

And now the transplant iris says
bloom time, petals in fours—bluish,
grayish blue, like silks
draped all over themselves.

Where Has the Day Gone?

You ate at your desk,

wrote notes for later, your last
glance out any window hours before.

Clouds arrived since then,

wind stilled—a day so late in the year
time of day by light is hard to say.

The copper beech is mossy and empty,

an aerial thicket that half reveals behind it
a brick wall fronted by steps

rising to twin, brown, and familiar doors
below a lantern-lit Palladian window.

Morning's dark walk to work: nine ages past

and two more to go, before you walk back
in the damp and the dark.

See

This is the person fond of peaches.
This is the person you know
Will not forgive.

This person watches the tide all day.
This person likes you afraid.
This person wakes thirsty

And this person fetches the water.
This person with nowhere to sleep
Sleeps where weariness decides.

This person practices with a chisel,
This with a needle,
This with a horsehair bow.

This person enjoys stomping in puddles.
This person loves dogs.
This person cannot stand straight.

This person's eyes open
And seeing you, they are pleased.

Notes & Acknowledgements

The Mary Barnard epigraph is from "Carillon," *Collected Poems*, Breitenbush Publications, 1979.

The Barry Lopez epigraph is from the Introduction to his book *About This Life*.

"Song of Bowl and Cup" is after John Yau's, "A Painter's Thoughts."

"A Margin of Trust" takes its title from Seamus Heaney's essay "W. B. Yeats and Thoor Ballylee."

"Life Is, Soberly and Accurately, the Oddest Affair" takes its title from Virginia Woolf's *A Writer's Diary*, entry for Sept. 30, 1926.

"This Crazy Old Home" takes its title from Mary Oliver's "Looking at a Book of van Gogh's Paintings, in Lewisburg, Pennsylvania" in her book *House of Light*.

"Neap Tide" is in memory of Bruce Edward Runciman.

"To Know This Your Home" is for Paulann Petersen and Ken Pallack.

The four photos referenced in "Eyes and Hand" were taken by Audrey Walker and are held in the archives of the Scottish National Gallery of Modern Art, Edinburgh.

The epigraphs for "Lines Composed after Four Days of Steady Rain" are drawn from the *Journals of Dorothy Wordsworth, Vol. 1*, edited by William Knight, 1897, 1904.

"Annunciations" is after Mary Szybist's *Incarnadine*.

Some of the poems in this book have not been published. Others have first appeared in the magazines and journals listed below. I am grateful to their editors, as follows:

Hubbub: "Words That Cannot Now Be Sung" and "What Do You Carry?"
Fireweed: "If the Forecast Holds."
Oregon Poetry Association Newsletter: "Letter to Rutsala from Sellwood."
Clackamas Literary Review: "Obsidian Snow" (originally "Broad River").
Windfall: "This Crazy Old Home" and section 2 of "Eventually You See Your Childhood."
Juxtaprose: "Reading the Autobiography of William Carlos Williams."
Praxis: "Unlooked For" and "Gold Beach."
Hotel Amerika: "Homage to Norman Maclean."
Dime Show Review: "Whiskey and a Slice of Pie."
LETTERS: "Seamus Heaney, St. Mary's, Bellaghy."
Camas (Linfield College): "Faltering Spring."

The Gettysburg Review: "Neap Tide."

Hole in the Head Review: "Eyes and Hand," "Himself," and "Ferry from Harris to Skye."

Whale Road Review: "On First Seeing a Photo of My Birth Mother."

Poetry Ireland Review: "News, 1949."

Slant: "Axis and Spin."

Keats-Shelley Review: "Keats."

Maine Review: "He Is Two and Does Not Want Shoes."

ONE, "View from the Night Stairs."

Valparaiso Poetry Review: "Looking for the Story Line" and "Hillside at Laugharne."

Verse-Virtual: "Picture Too Large to See," "Lines Composed after Four Days of Steady Rain," and "Life is, Soberly and Accurately, the Oddest Affair."

Poetry East: "A Watcher's Triptych"

Dreich: "Where Has the Day Gone?"

In addition, "What Do You Carry" appeared in *Hubbub* and was awarded the Vern Rutsala Prize. "Laundry" appeared in a special issue of *Valley Voices* edited by Philip Kolin on the theme of "Cotton." The first section of "Eventually You See Your Childhood" originally appeared in *Cloudbank* and is reprinted from *One Hour That Morning*. "Beach Walking, Early March, No Hat" and "Keeping it All" were finalists in the annual poetry contest sponsored by *Terrain*, and were subsequently published there. "Oranges Shared" appeared in *Coal Hill Review* and was nominated by its editors for *Best of the Net*. "Winter in the Pandemic Years" first appeared in the Oregon Poetry Association Pandemic Anthology, 2021. "Glance and Look Away" first appeared on the website of artist Ron Mills-Pinyas (www.mills-pinyas.com).

Special thanks to Jessie Lendennie and Siobhán Hutson Jeanotte for sustaining a vision and including me in it: congratulations to Salmon Poetry carrying on over 40 years. Special thanks to Paulann Petersen and Joe Wilkins for their responses to drafts; to Bill Siverly and Michael McDowell, for twenty years of *Windfall*; to Lisa Steinman and Jim Shugrue for thirty-four volumes of *Hubbub*; to Lee Bassett, maker of triptychs; and to Linfield College for opportunities to lead student travel courses in England, Wales, and Scotland. A book of poems owes many debts of gratitude, deeply felt if ill-expressed.

Most of the poems in this book were composed on the lands of the Multnomah, Clackamas, Kalapuya, Yaquina, and Alsea peoples, who lived with and on their ancestral lands from time immemorial. Their contemporary descendants have become the Confederated Tribes of the Grand Ronde Community of Oregon and the Confederated Tribes of the Siletz, who in their advocacies facilitate dialogue, maintain continuity, and provide protection of Tribal lifeways.

Photo: Sam Blair

LEX RUNCIMAN was born in Portland, Oregon's old St. Vincent's Hospital, adopted soon thereafter, and raised not far west of town. He graduated from Santa Clara University (B. A., 1973) and worked for two years as a warehouseman and shipping-receiving clerk before completing graduate study with Madeline DeFrees and Richard Hugo at the University of Montana (M.F.A., 1977), and with Dave Smith at the University of Utah (Ph.D., 1981).

He taught for 11 years at Oregon State University and then for 25 years at Linfield College, where he was twice named Edith Green Distinguished Professor. Runciman has co-edited two anthologies and co-authored three university textbooks. His poems have received the Kenneth O. Hanson Award, the Vern Rutsala Award, and the Silcox Prize. *The Admirations* won the Oregon Book Award in poetry. *One Hour That Morning* won the Julie Olds and Thomas Hellie Award for Creative Achievement.

Spouse to one, father of two, grandfather of four, he lives with his wife of 50 years in Portland, Oregon.

Unlooked For is his seventh collection of poems.

salmonpoetry

Cliffs of Moher, County Clare, Ireland

"Publishing the finest Irish and international literature."
Michael D. Higgins, President of Ireland